# *Begin the Day with Love & Gratitude*

*~ ~ ~*

*by Ash Azalea*

Creative Fusion Journals ©

Creative Fusion Journals ©

Copyright

Begin the Day with Love & Gratitude ©

By Ash Azalea

Creative Fusion Journals
Series 3 Edition 1

ISBN 9798683812546

Copyright © All rights Reserved.
No portion of this book may be reproduced or published in any form without the permission of the publisher, except as permitted by Copyright law. Please do not participate in or encourage piracy of copyrighted materials in violation of the authors rights. Purchase only authorized editions

Quotations in this Journal may be amended slightly from the original, but attribution remains.

Creative Fusion Journals ©

Creative Fusion Journals ©

*Take time each day to reflect on what or who you love and what you can be thankful for.*

*Sometimes, reflecting on the smallest of joys – a smile, sunshine, a song – can create the butterfly effect of helping you see the bigger joys of the world and your life.*

*These daily affirmations will help you develop your self-worth and live your life to it's potential – a potential that is uniquely yours.*

*Smile and the world smiles with you.*

Creative Fusion Journals ©

*Begin Your Day with Love & Gratitude*

> *In life, one has a choice to take one of two paths: to wait for some special day, or to celebrate each special day.*
> *Rasheed Ogunlaru*

Date .............................. I Love ...............................................

................................................................................................

I am thankful for ..............................................................

................................................................................................

Date .............................. I Love ...............................................

................................................................................................

I am thankful for ..............................................................

................................................................................................

Date .............................. I Love ...............................................

................................................................................................

I am thankful for ..............................................................

................................................................................................

Creative Fusion Journals ©

Date ………………………… I Love …………………………………...

………………………………………………………………………………..

I am thankful for ……………………………………………………..

………………………………………………………………………………..

Date ………………………… I Love …………………………………...

………………………………………………………………………………..

I am thankful for ……………………………………………………..

………………………………………………………………………………..

Date ………………………… I Love …………………………………...

………………………………………………………………………………..

I am thankful for ……………………………………………………..

………………………………………………………………………………..

Date ………………………… I Love …………………………………...

………………………………………………………………………………..

I am thankful for ……………………………………………………..

………………………………………………………………………………..

My Reflections on the week …………………………………………...

………………………………………………………………………………..

………………………………………………………………………………..

Creative Fusion Journals ©

*Begin Your Day with Love & Gratitude*

> *Gratitude and attitude are not challenges; they are choices. –*
> *Robert Braathe*

Date ............................... *I Love* ..............................................

..................................................................................................

*I am thankful for* ...............................................................

..................................................................................................

Date ............................... *I Love* ..............................................

..................................................................................................

*I am thankful for* ...............................................................

..................................................................................................

Date ............................... *I Love* ..............................................

..................................................................................................

*I am thankful for* ...............................................................

..................................................................................................

Creative Fusion Journals ©

Date .................................. I Love ...............................................

...................................................................................................

I am thankful for ...............................................................

...................................................................................................

Date .................................. I Love ...............................................

...................................................................................................

I am thankful for ...............................................................

...................................................................................................

Date .................................. I Love ...............................................

...................................................................................................

I am thankful for ...............................................................

...................................................................................................

Date .................................. I Love ...............................................

...................................................................................................

I am thankful for ...............................................................

...................................................................................................

My Reflections on the week ...............................................

...................................................................................................

...................................................................................................

Creative Fusion Journals ©

## Begin Your Day with Love & Gratitude

> *Gratitude opens your eyes to the limitless potential of the universe, while dissatisfaction closes your eyes to it.*
> *Stephen Richards*

Date ............................... I Love ..............................................

..............................................................................................

I am thankful for ...........................................................

..............................................................................................

Date ............................... I Love ..............................................

..............................................................................................

I am thankful for ...........................................................

..............................................................................................

Date ............................... I Love ..............................................

..............................................................................................

I am thankful for ...........................................................

..............................................................................................

Creative Fusion Journals ©

*Date* .................................. *I Love* ..............................................

.. ...........................................................................................................

*I am thankful for* ...........................................................................

...........................................................................................................

*Date* .................................. *I Love* ..............................................

.. ...........................................................................................................

*I am thankful for* ...........................................................................

...........................................................................................................

*Date* .................................. *I Love* ..............................................

...........................................................................................................

*I am thankful for* ...........................................................................

.. ...........................................................................................................

*Date* .................................. *I Love* ..............................................

.. ...........................................................................................................

*I am thankful for* ...........................................................................

...........................................................................................................

*My Reflections on the week* ........................................................

...........................................................................................................

...........................................................................................................

Creative Fusion Journals ©

## Begin Your Day with Love & Gratitude

> *Acknowledging the good you already have in your life is the foundation for all abundance.*
> *Eckhart Tolle*

Date ............................... I Love ................................................

................................................................................................

I am thankful for ................................................................

................................................................................................


Date ............................... I Love ................................................

................................................................................................

I am thankful for ................................................................

................................................................................................


Date ............................... I Love ................................................

................................................................................................

I am thankful for ................................................................

................................................................................................


Creative Fusion Journals ©

Date ............................... I Love .............................................

...................................................................................................

I am thankful for .............................................................

...................................................................................................

Date ............................... I Love .............................................

...................................................................................................

I am thankful for .............................................................

...................................................................................................

Date ............................... I Love .............................................

...................................................................................................

I am thankful for .............................................................

...................................................................................................

Date ............................... I Love .............................................

...................................................................................................

I am thankful for .............................................................

...................................................................................................

My Reflections on the week .................................................

...................................................................................................

...................................................................................................

Creative Fusion Journals ©

## Begin Your Day with Love & Gratitude

> *Where there is no struggle, there is no strength.*
> *Oprah Winfrey*

Date .............................. I Love ..................................................

..............................................................................................

I am thankful for ......................................................................

..............................................................................................

Date .............................. I Love ..................................................

..............................................................................................

I am thankful for ......................................................................

..............................................................................................

Date .............................. I Love ..................................................

..............................................................................................

I am thankful for ......................................................................

..............................................................................................

Creative Fusion Journals ©

Date ................................. I Love ............................................
..............................................................................................................
I am thankful for ..........................................................................
..............................................................................................................

Date ................................. I Love ............................................
..............................................................................................................
I am thankful for ..........................................................................
..............................................................................................................

Date ................................. I Love ............................................
..............................................................................................................
I am thankful for ..........................................................................
..............................................................................................................

Date ................................. I Love ............................................
..............................................................................................................
I am thankful for ..........................................................................
..............................................................................................................
My Reflections on the week ........................................................
..............................................................................................................
..............................................................................................................

Creative Fusion Journals ©

## Begin Your Day with Love & Gratitude

> *Do not judge me by my successes, judge me by how many times I fell down and got back up.*
> *Nelson Mandela*

Date ............................... I Love ...............................................

..................................................................................................

I am thankful for ..............................................................................

..................................................................................................

Date ............................... I Love ...............................................

..................................................................................................

I am thankful for ..............................................................................

..................................................................................................

Date ............................... I Love ...............................................

..................................................................................................

I am thankful for ..............................................................................

..................................................................................................

Creative Fusion Journals ©

*Date* ............................... *I Love* ...............................................

...................................................................................................

*I am thankful for* ...............................................................................

...................................................................................................

*Date* ............................... *I Love* ...............................................

...................................................................................................

*I am thankful for* ...............................................................................

...................................................................................................

*Date* ............................... *I Love* ...............................................

...................................................................................................

*I am thankful for* ...............................................................................

...................................................................................................

*Date* ............................... *I Love* ...............................................

...................................................................................................

*I am thankful for* ...............................................................................

...................................................................................................

*My Reflections on the week* ...................................................................

...................................................................................................

...................................................................................................

Creative Fusion Journals ©

# Begin Your Day with Love & Gratitude

> *Turn your wounds into wisdom.*
> Oprah Winfrey

Date ............................... I Love ...................................................

..................................................................................................

I am thankful for ............................................................................

..................................................................................................


Date ............................... I Love ...................................................

..................................................................................................

I am thankful for ............................................................................

..................................................................................................


Date ............................... I Love ...................................................

..................................................................................................

I am thankful for ............................................................................

..................................................................................................

Creative Fusion Journals ©

Date .................................. I Love .................................................

....................................................................................................

I am thankful for ...................................................................

....................................................................................................

Date .................................. I Love .................................................

....................................................................................................

I am thankful for ...................................................................

....................................................................................................

Date .................................. I Love .................................................

....................................................................................................

I am thankful for ...................................................................

....................................................................................................

Date .................................. I Love .................................................

....................................................................................................

I am thankful for ...................................................................

....................................................................................................

My Reflections on the week .......................................................

....................................................................................................

....................................................................................................

Creative Fusion Journals ©

# Begin Your Day with Love & Gratitude

> *Seek first to understand and then be understood.*
> *Stephen R. Covey*

Date ............................... I Love ..............................................

..................................................................................................

I am thankful for ...................................................................

..................................................................................................


Date ............................... I Love ..............................................

..................................................................................................

I am thankful for ...................................................................

..................................................................................................


Date ............................... I Love ..............................................

..................................................................................................

I am thankful for ...................................................................

..................................................................................................


Creative Fusion Journals ©

Date ............................... I Love ...........................................

..............................................................................................

I am thankful for ...................................................................

..............................................................................................

Date ............................... I Love ...........................................

..............................................................................................

I am thankful for ...................................................................

..............................................................................................

Date ............................... I Love ...........................................

..............................................................................................

I am thankful for ...................................................................

..............................................................................................

Date ............................... I Love ...........................................

..............................................................................................

I am thankful for ...................................................................

..............................................................................................

My Reflections on the week .....................................................

..............................................................................................

..............................................................................................

Creative Fusion Journals ©

## Begin Your Day with Love & Gratitude

> *At times, our own light goes out and is rekindled by another. Each of us has cause to think with deep gratitude of those who have lit a flame within us.*
> Albert Schweitzer

Date .............................. I Love ..............................................

..........................................................................................

I am thankful for ..................................................................

..........................................................................................

Date .............................. I Love ..............................................

..........................................................................................

I am thankful for ..................................................................

..........................................................................................

Date .............................. I Love ..............................................

..........................................................................................

I am thankful for ..................................................................

..........................................................................................

Creative Fusion Journals ©

Date .................................... I Love ...............................................

.. ................................................................................................

I am thankful for ..............................................................................

.. ...............................................................................................

Date .................................... I Love ...............................................

.. ...............................................................................................

I am thankful for ..............................................................................

.. ...............................................................................................

Date .................................... I Love ...............................................

.. ...............................................................................................

I am thankful for ..............................................................................

.. ...............................................................................................

Date .................................... I Love ...............................................

.. ...............................................................................................

I am thankful for ..............................................................................

.. ...............................................................................................

My Reflections on the week ...............................................................

.. ...............................................................................................

.. ...............................................................................................

Creative Fusion Journals ©

# Begin Your Day with Love & Gratitude

> *It is a wise person who does not grieve for the things they do not have, but rejoices for that which they have.*
> *Epictetus*

Date ............................... I Love ...............................................

..............................................................................................

I am thankful for ......................................................................

..............................................................................................

Date ............................... I Love ...............................................

..............................................................................................

I am thankful for ......................................................................

..............................................................................................

Date ............................... I Love ...............................................

..............................................................................................

I am thankful for ......................................................................

..............................................................................................

Creative Fusion Journals ©

*Date* .............................. *I Love* ..............................................

............................................................................................................

*I am thankful for* ...........................................................................

............................................................................................................

*Date* .............................. *I Love* ..............................................

............................................................................................................

*I am thankful for* ...........................................................................

............................................................................................................

*Date* .............................. *I Love* ..............................................

............................................................................................................

*I am thankful for* ...........................................................................

............................................................................................................

*Date* .............................. *I Love* ..............................................

............................................................................................................

*I am thankful for* ...........................................................................

............................................................................................................

*My Reflections on the week* ...........................................................

............................................................................................................

............................................................................................................

Creative Fusion Journals ©

## Begin Your Day with Love & Gratitude

> *Gratitude is a currency we can mint for ourselves and spend without fear of bankruptcy.*
> F. De Witt Van Amburgh

Date .................................. I Love ...............................................

........................................................................................................

I am thankful for ................................................................................

........................................................................................................

Date .................................. I Love ...............................................

........................................................................................................

I am thankful for ................................................................................

........................................................................................................

Date .................................. I Love ...............................................

........................................................................................................

I am thankful for ................................................................................

........................................................................................................

Creative Fusion Journals ©

Date ................................ I Love ..............................................

..................................................................................................

I am thankful for ..................................................................

..................................................................................................

Date ................................ I Love ..............................................

..................................................................................................

I am thankful for ..................................................................

..................................................................................................

Date ................................ I Love ..............................................

..................................................................................................

I am thankful for ..................................................................

..................................................................................................

Date ................................ I Love ..............................................

..................................................................................................

I am thankful for ..................................................................

..................................................................................................

My Reflections on the week ................................................

..................................................................................................

..................................................................................................

Creative Fusion Journals ©

## Begin Your Day with Love & Gratitude

> *Gratitude... makes sense of our past, brings peace for today and creates a vision for tomorrow.*
> *Melody Beattie*

Date .................................. I Love ................................................

................................................................................................

I am thankful for .....................................................................

................................................................................................

Date .................................. I Love ................................................

................................................................................................

I am thankful for .....................................................................

................................................................................................

Date .................................. I Love ................................................

................................................................................................

I am thankful for .....................................................................

................................................................................................

Date ............................... I Love ................................................

............................................................................................

I am thankful for ............................................................

............................................................................................

Date ............................... I Love ................................................

............................................................................................

I am thankful for ............................................................

............................................................................................

Date ............................... I Love ................................................

............................................................................................

I am thankful for ............................................................

............................................................................................

Date ............................... I Love ................................................

............................................................................................

I am thankful for ............................................................

............................................................................................

My Reflections on the week ....................................................

............................................................................................

............................................................................................

Creative Fusion Journals ©

## Begin Your Day with Love & Gratitude

> *Let your choices reflect your hopes, not your fears.*
> *Nelson Mandela*

Date ............................... I Love ................................................

..............................................................................................

I am thankful for ......................................................................

..............................................................................................

Date ............................... I Love ................................................

..............................................................................................

I am thankful for ......................................................................

..............................................................................................

Date ............................... I Love ................................................

..............................................................................................

I am thankful for ......................................................................

..............................................................................................

Creative Fusion Journals ©

Date ………………………… I Love ……………………………………..

………………………………………………………………………………..

I am thankful for …………………………………………………………..

………………………………………………………………………………..

Date ………………………… I Love ……………………………………..

………………………………………………………………………………..

I am thankful for …………………………………………………………..

………………………………………………………………………………..

Date ………………………… I Love ……………………………………..

………………………………………………………………………………..

I am thankful for …………………………………………………………..

………………………………………………………………………………..

Date ………………………… I Love ……………………………………..

………………………………………………………………………………..

I am thankful for …………………………………………………………..

………………………………………………………………………………..

My Reflections on the week …………………………………………...

………………………………………………………………………………..

………………………………………………………………………………..

Creative Fusion Journals ©

# Begin Your Day with Love & Gratitude

> *A winner is a dreamer who never gives up.*
> Nelson Mandela

Date ................................. I Love ...............................................

......................................................................................................

I am thankful for ............................................................................

......................................................................................................

Date ................................. I Love ...............................................

......................................................................................................

I am thankful for ............................................................................

......................................................................................................

Date ................................. I Love ...............................................

......................................................................................................

I am thankful for ............................................................................

......................................................................................................

Creative Fusion Journals ©

Date ............................... I Love ...............................................

..............................................................................................

I am thankful for ........................................................................

..............................................................................................

Date ............................... I Love ...............................................

..............................................................................................

I am thankful for ........................................................................

..............................................................................................

Date ............................... I Love ...............................................

..............................................................................................

I am thankful for ........................................................................

..............................................................................................

Date ............................... I Love ...............................................

..............................................................................................

I am thankful for ........................................................................

..............................................................................................

My Reflections on the week ........................................................

..............................................................................................

..............................................................................................

Creative Fusion Journals ©

# Begin Your Day with Love & Gratitude

> *Be kind whenever possible. It is always possible.*
> *Dalai Lama*

Date .............................. I Love ..............................................

..................................................................................................

I am thankful for ......................................................................

..................................................................................................

Date .............................. I Love ..............................................

..................................................................................................

I am thankful for ......................................................................

..................................................................................................

Date .............................. I Love ..............................................

..................................................................................................

I am thankful for ......................................................................

..................................................................................................

Creative Fusion Journals ©

Date ............................... I Love ..............................................

..................................................................................................

I am thankful for ...............................................................

..................................................................................................

Date ............................... I Love ..............................................

..................................................................................................

I am thankful for ...............................................................

..................................................................................................

Date ............................... I Love ..............................................

..................................................................................................

I am thankful for ...............................................................

..................................................................................................

Date ............................... I Love ..............................................

..................................................................................................

I am thankful for ...............................................................

..................................................................................................

My Reflections on the week ...............................................

..................................................................................................

..................................................................................................

Creative Fusion Journals ©

## Begin Your Day with Love & Gratitude

> *Kind words can be short and easy to speak; but their echoes are truly endless.* – Mother Theresa

Date ............................... I Love ...............................................

..........................................................................................................

I am thankful for ..................................................................................

..........................................................................................................

Date ............................... I Love ...............................................

..........................................................................................................

I am thankful for ..................................................................................

..........................................................................................................

Date ............................... I Love ...............................................

..........................................................................................................

I am thankful for ..................................................................................

..........................................................................................................

Creative Fusion Journals ©

Date .................................. I Love ...............................................

................................................................................................

I am thankful for ..............................................................

................................................................................................

Date .................................. I Love ...............................................

................................................................................................

I am thankful for ..............................................................

................................................................................................

Date .................................. I Love ...............................................

................................................................................................

I am thankful for ..............................................................

................................................................................................

Date .................................. I Love ...............................................

................................................................................................

I am thankful for ..............................................................

................................................................................................

My Reflections on the week ...........................................................

................................................................................................

................................................................................................

Creative Fusion Journals ©

# Begin Your Day with Love & Gratitude

> *Do not wait for leaders. Do it alone, person to person.*
> *Mother Theresa*

Date ............................... I Love ...............................................

..........................................................................................................

I am thankful for ...................................................................................

..........................................................................................................


Date ............................... I Love ...............................................

..........................................................................................................

I am thankful for ...................................................................................

..........................................................................................................


Date ............................... I Love ...............................................

..........................................................................................................

I am thankful for ...................................................................................

..........................................................................................................


Creative Fusion Journals ©

Date ………………………… I Love …………………………………...

……………………………………………………………………………..

I am thankful for …………………………………………………...

……………………………………………………………………………..

Date ………………………… I Love …………………………………...

……………………………………………………………………………..

I am thankful for …………………………………………………...

……………………………………………………………………………..

Date ………………………… I Love …………………………………...

……………………………………………………………………………..

I am thankful for …………………………………………………...

……………………………………………………………………………..

Date ………………………… I Love …………………………………...

……………………………………………………………………………..

I am thankful for …………………………………………………...

……………………………………………………………………………..

My Reflections on the week …………………………………………...

……………………………………………………………………………..

……………………………………………………………………………..

Creative Fusion Journals ©

# Begin Your Day with Love & Gratitude

> *Wherever you go, go with all your heart.*
> *Confucius*

Date ............................... I Love .............................................

...................................................................................................

I am thankful for ..........................................................................

...................................................................................................

Date ............................... I Love .............................................

...................................................................................................

I am thankful for ..........................................................................

...................................................................................................

Date ............................... I Love .............................................

...................................................................................................

I am thankful for ..........................................................................

...................................................................................................

Creative Fusion Journals ©

Date ................................. I Love ...............................................

..............................................................................................................

I am thankful for ............................................................................

..............................................................................................................

Date ................................. I Love ...............................................

..............................................................................................................

I am thankful for ............................................................................

..............................................................................................................

Date ................................. I Love ...............................................

..............................................................................................................

I am thankful for ............................................................................

..............................................................................................................

Date ................................. I Love ...............................................

..............................................................................................................

I am thankful for ............................................................................

..............................................................................................................

My Reflections on the week ........................................................

..............................................................................................................

..............................................................................................................

Creative Fusion Journals ©

*Begin Your Day with Love & Gratitude*

> *Courage is not the absence of fear; but triumph over it.*
> *Nelson Mandela*

Date .............................. *I Love* ..............................................

..................................................................................................

*I am thankful for* ...................................................................

..................................................................................................


Date .............................. *I Love* ..............................................

..................................................................................................

*I am thankful for* ...................................................................

..................................................................................................


Date .............................. *I Love* ..............................................

..................................................................................................

*I am thankful for* ...................................................................

..................................................................................................

Creative Fusion Journals ©

Date ................................ I Love ..............................................

..................................................................................................

I am thankful for .......................................................................

..................................................................................................

Date ................................ I Love ..............................................

..................................................................................................

I am thankful for .......................................................................

..................................................................................................

Date ................................ I Love ..............................................

..................................................................................................

I am thankful for .......................................................................

..................................................................................................

Date ................................ I Love ..............................................

..................................................................................................

I am thankful for .......................................................................

..................................................................................................

My Reflections on the week ........................................................

..................................................................................................

..................................................................................................

Creative Fusion Journals ©

## Begin Your Day with Love & Gratitude

> *Have courage to do what is right; you know what is right.*
> *This is a route to inner peace.*
> *Ash Azalea*

Date ............................... I Love ..............................................

................................................................................................

I am thankful for ..................................................................

................................................................................................

Date ............................... I Love ..............................................

................................................................................................

I am thankful for ..................................................................

................................................................................................

Date ............................... I Love ..............................................

................................................................................................

I am thankful for ..................................................................

................................................................................................

Creative Fusion Journals ©

*Date* ................................. *I Love* .............................................

..............................................................................................

*I am thankful for* ..............................................................

..............................................................................................

*Date* ................................. *I Love* .............................................

..............................................................................................

*I am thankful for* ..............................................................

..............................................................................................

*Date* ................................. *I Love* .............................................

..............................................................................................

*I am thankful for* ..............................................................

..............................................................................................

*Date* ................................. *I Love* .............................................

..............................................................................................

*I am thankful for* ..............................................................

..............................................................................................

*My Reflections on the week* ...........................................

..............................................................................................

..............................................................................................

Creative Fusion Journals ©

## Begin Your Day with Love & Gratitude

> *Things turn out best for people who make the best of the way things turn out.*
> *John Wooden*

Date ............................... I Love ................................................

..................................................................................................

I am thankful for ...........................................................................

..................................................................................................

Date ............................... I Love ................................................

..................................................................................................

I am thankful for ...........................................................................

..................................................................................................

Date ............................... I Love ................................................

..................................................................................................

I am thankful for ...........................................................................

..................................................................................................

Creative Fusion Journals ©

Date ............................... I Love ...........................................
................................................................................................

I am thankful for ....................................................................

................................................................................................

Date ............................... I Love ...........................................
................................................................................................

I am thankful for ....................................................................

................................................................................................

Date ............................... I Love ...........................................
................................................................................................

I am thankful for ....................................................................

................................................................................................

Date ............................... I Love ...........................................
................................................................................................

I am thankful for ....................................................................

................................................................................................

My Reflections on the week ............................................................

................................................................................................

................................................................................................

Creative Fusion Journals ©

## Begin Your Day with Love & Gratitude

> *You are the Captain of your soul.*
> *Nelson Mandela*

Date ............................... I Love ...............................................

..........................................................................................................

I am thankful for ............................................................................

..........................................................................................................

Date ............................... I Love ...............................................

..........................................................................................................

I am thankful for ............................................................................

..........................................................................................................

Date ............................... I Love ...............................................

..........................................................................................................

I am thankful for ............................................................................

..........................................................................................................

Creative Fusion Journals ©

Date ................................. I Love ................................................…..

………………………………………………………………………………………………..

I am thankful for ………………………………………………………………………..

………………………………………………………………………………………………..

Date ................................. I Love ................................................…..

………………………………………………………………………………………………..

I am thankful for ………………………………………………………………………..

………………………………………………………………………………………………..

Date ................................. I Love ................................................…..

………………………………………………………………………………………………..

I am thankful for ………………………………………………………………………..

………………………………………………………………………………………………..

Date ................................. I Love ................................................…..

………………………………………………………………………………………………..

I am thankful for ………………………………………………………………………..

………………………………………………………………………………………………..

My Reflections on the week ………………………………………………………...

………………………………………………………………………………………………..

………………………………………………………………………………………………..

Creative Fusion Journals ©

*Begin Your Day with Love & Gratitude*

> *Enjoy the little things, for one day you will look back and realize they were the big things.*
> *Robert Brault*

Date .................................. I Love ...............................................

..........................................................................................................

I am thankful for ....................................................................

..........................................................................................................

Date .................................. I Love ...............................................

..........................................................................................................

I am thankful for ....................................................................

..........................................................................................................

Date .................................. I Love ...............................................

..........................................................................................................

I am thankful for ....................................................................

..........................................................................................................

Creative Fusion Journals ©

*Date* ............................... *I Love* ................................................

............................................................................................

*I am thankful for* ....................................................................

............................................................................................

*Date* ............................... *I Love* ................................................

............................................................................................

*I am thankful for* ....................................................................

............................................................................................

*Date* ............................... *I Love* ................................................

............................................................................................

*I am thankful for* ....................................................................

............................................................................................

*Date* ............................... *I Love* ................................................

............................................................................................

*I am thankful for* ....................................................................

............................................................................................

*My Reflections on the week* ....................................................

............................................................................................

............................................................................................

Creative Fusion Journals ©

## Begin Your Day with Love & Gratitude

> *Reflect upon your present blessings, of which every person has plenty, not on past misfortunes, of which every person has some.*
> *Charles Dickens*

Date ............................... I Love .............................................
..............................................................................................
I am thankful for ......................................................................
..............................................................................................

Date ............................... I Love .............................................
..............................................................................................
I am thankful for ......................................................................
..............................................................................................

Date ............................... I Love .............................................
..............................................................................................
I am thankful for ......................................................................
..............................................................................................

Creative Fusion Journals ©

Date .................................. I Love ...............................................

..................................................................................................

I am thankful for ...............................................................

..................................................................................................

Date .................................. I Love ...............................................

..................................................................................................

I am thankful for ...............................................................

..................................................................................................

Date .................................. I Love ...............................................

..................................................................................................

I am thankful for ...............................................................

..................................................................................................

Date .................................. I Love ...............................................

..................................................................................................

I am thankful for ...............................................................

..................................................................................................

My Reflections on the week ...................................................

..................................................................................................

..................................................................................................

Creative Fusion Journals ©

## Begin Your Day with Love & Gratitude

> *Gratitude… the highest appreciation is not to utter words, but to live by them.*
> *John F Kennedy*

Date ............................... I Love ...............................................

..........................................................................................

I am thankful for ...................................................................

..........................................................................................

Date ............................... I Love ...............................................

..........................................................................................

I am thankful for ...................................................................

..........................................................................................

Date ............................... I Love ...............................................

..........................................................................................

I am thankful for ...................................................................

..........................................................................................

Creative Fusion Journals ©

Date ................................. I Love ................................................

............................................................................................................

I am thankful for ...............................................................................

............................................................................................................

Date ................................. I Love ................................................

............................................................................................................

I am thankful for ...............................................................................

............................................................................................................

Date ................................. I Love ................................................

............................................................................................................

I am thankful for ...............................................................................

............................................................................................................

Date ................................. I Love ................................................

............................................................................................................

I am thankful for ...............................................................................

............................................................................................................

My Reflections on the week ................................................................

............................................................................................................

............................................................................................................

Creative Fusion Journals ©

## Begin Your Day with Love & Gratitude

> *We receive a great deal more than we give, and it is only with gratitude that life becomes rich.*
> *Dietrich Bonhoeffer*

Date .................................. I Love ................................................

............................................................................................................

I am thankful for ..................................................................................

............................................................................................................

Date .................................. I Love ................................................

............................................................................................................

I am thankful for ..................................................................................

............................................................................................................

Date .................................. I Love ................................................

............................................................................................................

I am thankful for ..................................................................................

............................................................................................................

Creative Fusion Journals ©

Date ................................. I Love ...............................................

................................................................................................

I am thankful for ................................................................

................................................................................................

Date ................................. I Love ...............................................

................................................................................................

I am thankful for ................................................................

................................................................................................

Date ................................. I Love ...............................................

................................................................................................

I am thankful for ................................................................

................................................................................................

Date ................................. I Love ...............................................

................................................................................................

I am thankful for ................................................................

................................................................................................

My Reflections on the week ...............................................................

................................................................................................

................................................................................................

Creative Fusion Journals ©

*Begin Your Day with Love & Gratitude*

> *We do not need to change the world, or even ourselves. Just accept, embrace & share the love within us.*
> *Harold W Becker*

Date ............................... I Love ...............................................

..................................................................................................

I am thankful for ...............................................................

..................................................................................................

Date ............................... I Love ...............................................

..................................................................................................

I am thankful for ...............................................................

..................................................................................................

Date ............................... I Love ...............................................

..................................................................................................

I am thankful for ...............................................................

..................................................................................................

Creative Fusion Journals ©

*Date* ............................... *I Love* ..............................................

..................................................................................................

*I am thankful for* ................................................................

..................................................................................................

*Date* ............................... *I Love* ..............................................

..................................................................................................

*I am thankful for* ................................................................

..................................................................................................

*Date* ............................... *I Love* ..............................................

..................................................................................................

*I am thankful for* ................................................................

..................................................................................................

*Date* ............................... *I Love* ..............................................

..................................................................................................

*I am thankful for* ................................................................

..................................................................................................

*My Reflections on the week* ..............................................

..................................................................................................

..................................................................................................

Creative Fusion Journals ©

## Begin Your Day with Love & Gratitude

> *Peoples expectations of you, are their problem, not yours. Honor your individuality.*
> *Anon*

Date ........................... I Love ...........................................

..................................................................................................

I am thankful for ..................................................................

..................................................................................................

Date ........................... I Love ...........................................

..................................................................................................

I am thankful for ..................................................................

..................................................................................................

Date ........................... I Love ...........................................

..................................................................................................

I am thankful for ..................................................................

..................................................................................................

Creative Fusion Journals ©

*Date* .............................. *I Love* ..............................................

..................................................................................................

*I am thankful for* ...................................................................

..................................................................................................

*Date* .............................. *I Love* ..............................................

..................................................................................................

*I am thankful for* ...................................................................

..................................................................................................

*Date* .............................. *I Love* ..............................................

..................................................................................................

*I am thankful for* ...................................................................

..................................................................................................

*Date* .............................. *I Love* ..............................................

..................................................................................................

*I am thankful for* ...................................................................

..................................................................................................

*My Reflections on the week* ....................................................

..................................................................................................

..................................................................................................

Creative Fusion Journals ©

# Begin Your Day with Love & Gratitude

> *Forgiveness is the attribute of the strong.*
> *Mahatma Gandhi*

Date ............................... I Love ..............................................

............................................................................................

I am thankful for ........................................................................

............................................................................................

Date ............................... I Love ..............................................

............................................................................................

I am thankful for ........................................................................

............................................................................................

Date ............................... I Love ..............................................

............................................................................................

I am thankful for ........................................................................

............................................................................................

Creative Fusion Journals ©

Date ............................... I Love ..............................................

................................................................................................

I am thankful for ...........................................................

................................................................................................

Date ............................... I Love ..............................................

................................................................................................

I am thankful for ...........................................................

................................................................................................

Date ............................... I Love ..............................................

................................................................................................

I am thankful for ...........................................................

................................................................................................

Date ............................... I Love ..............................................

................................................................................................

I am thankful for ...........................................................

................................................................................................

My Reflections on the week ............................................

................................................................................................

................................................................................................

Creative Fusion Journals ©

# Begin Your Day with Love & Gratitude

> *Accept no one's definition of your life; define yourself.*
> *Harvey Fierstein*

Date .............................. I Love ..............................

..............................................................................

I am thankful for ..............................................................

..............................................................................

Date .............................. I Love ..............................

..............................................................................

I am thankful for ..............................................................

..............................................................................

Date .............................. I Love ..............................

..............................................................................

I am thankful for ..............................................................

..............................................................................

Creative Fusion Journals ©

*Date* ............................... *I Love* ...............................................

.... ..................................................................................................

*I am thankful for* ...................................................................

.... ..................................................................................................


*Date* ............................... *I Love* ...............................................

.... ..................................................................................................

*I am thankful for* ...................................................................

..........................................................................................................


*Date* ............................... *I Love* ...............................................

..........................................................................................................

*I am thankful for* ...................................................................

..........................................................................................................


*Date* ............................... *I Love* ...............................................

..........................................................................................................

*I am thankful for* ...................................................................

..........................................................................................................

*My Reflections on the week* ...................................................

..........................................................................................................

..........................................................................................................

Creative Fusion Journals ©

*Begin Your Day with Love & Gratitude*

---

*Take Action. You will rarely regret what you have done, but more likely regret what you didn't do.*
*Ash Azalea*

---

Date ................................. I Love ...............................................

................................................................................................

I am thankful for ...........................................................................

................................................................................................


Date ................................. I Love ...............................................

................................................................................................

I am thankful for ...........................................................................

................................................................................................


Date ................................. I Love ...............................................

................................................................................................

I am thankful for ...........................................................................

................................................................................................

Creative Fusion Journals ©

*Date* ........................... *I Love* ..........................................

..................................................................................................

*I am thankful for* ................................................................

..................................................................................................

*Date* ........................... *I Love* ..........................................

..................................................................................................

*I am thankful for* ................................................................

..................................................................................................

*Date* ........................... *I Love* ..........................................

..................................................................................................

*I am thankful for* ................................................................

..................................................................................................

*Date* ........................... *I Love* ..........................................

..................................................................................................

*I am thankful for* ................................................................

..................................................................................................

*My Reflections on the week* ................................................

..................................................................................................

..................................................................................................

Creative Fusion Journals ©

## Begin Your Day with Love & Gratitude

> *Do not overestimate the competition and underestimate yourself.*
> *You are better than you think.*
> *T Harv Ecker*

Date .............................. I Love ..............................................

..........................................................................................

I am thankful for ....................................................................

..........................................................................................


Date .............................. I Love ..............................................

..........................................................................................

I am thankful for ....................................................................

..........................................................................................


Date .............................. I Love ..............................................

..........................................................................................

I am thankful for ....................................................................

..........................................................................................


Creative Fusion Journals ©

*Date* .................................. *I Love* ..............................................
..................................................................................................
*I am thankful for* ..........................................................................
..................................................................................................

*Date* .................................. *I Love* ..............................................
..................................................................................................
*I am thankful for* ..........................................................................
..................................................................................................

*Date* .................................. *I Love* ..............................................
..................................................................................................
*I am thankful for* ..........................................................................
..................................................................................................

*Date* .................................. *I Love* ..............................................
..................................................................................................
*I am thankful for* ..........................................................................
..................................................................................................
*My Reflections on the week* ............................................................
..................................................................................................
..................................................................................................

Creative Fusion Journals ©

## Begin Your Day with Love & Gratitude

> *Be happy with what you have. Be excited with what you want. - Alan Cohen*

Date .............................. I Love ..............................................

................................................................................................

I am thankful for ......................................................................

................................................................................................

Date .............................. I Love ..............................................

................................................................................................

I am thankful for ......................................................................

................................................................................................

Date .............................. I Love ..............................................

................................................................................................

I am thankful for ......................................................................

................................................................................................

Creative Fusion Journals ©

*Date* .................................. *I Love* ..............................................

..................................................................................................

*I am thankful for* ...............................................................

..................................................................................................

*Date* .................................. *I Love* ..............................................

..................................................................................................

*I am thankful for* ...............................................................

..................................................................................................

*Date* .................................. *I Love* ..............................................

..................................................................................................

*I am thankful for* ...............................................................

..................................................................................................

*Date* .................................. *I Love* ..............................................

..................................................................................................

*I am thankful for* ...............................................................

..................................................................................................

*My Reflections on the week* .............................................

..................................................................................................

..................................................................................................

Creative Fusion Journals ©

## Begin Your Day with Love & Gratitude

> *Happiness is not a goal; it is the reward.*
> *Ash Azalea*

Date ............................... I Love ..............................................

..........................................................................................

I am thankful for ....................................................................

..........................................................................................

Date ............................... I Love ..............................................

..........................................................................................

I am thankful for ....................................................................

..........................................................................................

Date ............................... I Love ..............................................

..........................................................................................

I am thankful for ....................................................................

..........................................................................................

Creative Fusion Journals ©

Date …………………………… I Love ………………………………………..

……………………………………………………………………………………..

I am thankful for …………………………………………………………………..

……………………………………………………………………………………..


Date …………………………… I Love ………………………………………..

……………………………………………………………………………………..

I am thankful for …………………………………………………………………..

……………………………………………………………………………………..


Date …………………………… I Love ………………………………………..

……………………………………………………………………………………..

I am thankful for …………………………………………………………………..

……………………………………………………………………………………..


Date …………………………… I Love ………………………………………..

……………………………………………………………………………………..

I am thankful for …………………………………………………………………..

……………………………………………………………………………………..

My Reflections on the week …………………………………………………….

……………………………………………………………………………………..

……………………………………………………………………………………..

Creative Fusion Journals ©

# Begin Your Day with Love & Gratitude

> *'Happy' would lose its meaning if it were not balanced by sadness. Take things as they come with patience and equanimity.*
> *Carl Jung*

Date ............................... I Love ...........................................

...........................................................................................

I am thankful for ...................................................................

...........................................................................................

Date ............................... I Love ...........................................

...........................................................................................

I am thankful for ...................................................................

...........................................................................................

Date ............................... I Love ...........................................

...........................................................................................

I am thankful for ...................................................................

...........................................................................................

Creative Fusion Journals ©

*Date* .................................. *I Love* ..............................................

..................................................................................................

*I am thankful for* ...................................................................

..................................................................................................

*Date* .................................. *I Love* ..............................................

..................................................................................................

*I am thankful for* ...................................................................

..................................................................................................

*Date* .................................. *I Love* ..............................................

..................................................................................................

*I am thankful for* ...................................................................

..................................................................................................

*Date* .................................. *I Love* ..............................................

..................................................................................................

*I am thankful for* ...................................................................

..................................................................................................

*My Reflections on the week* ...................................................

..................................................................................................

..................................................................................................

Creative Fusion Journals ©

# Begin Your Day with Love & Gratitude

> *The secret of happiness is freedom, the secret of freedom is courage.*
> *Carrie Francis*

Date ............................... I Love ...............................................

..........................................................................................

I am thankful for ....................................................................

..........................................................................................

Date ............................... I Love ...............................................

..........................................................................................

I am thankful for ....................................................................

..........................................................................................

Date ............................... I Love ...............................................

..........................................................................................

I am thankful for ....................................................................

..........................................................................................

Creative Fusion Journals ©

*Date* .............................. *I Love* ..............................................
..................................................................................................

*I am thankful for* ...............................................................
..................................................................................................

*Date* .............................. *I Love* ..............................................
..................................................................................................

*I am thankful for* ...............................................................
..................................................................................................

*Date* .............................. *I Love* ..............................................
..................................................................................................

*I am thankful for* ...............................................................
..................................................................................................

*Date* .............................. *I Love* ..............................................
..................................................................................................

*I am thankful for* ...............................................................
..................................................................................................

*My Reflections on the week* ..................................................
..................................................................................................
..................................................................................................

Creative Fusion Journals ©

# Begin Your Day with Love & Gratitude

> *If you want happiness for a lifetime, help someone else.*
> *Anon*

Date .................................. I Love ................................................

..........................................................................................................

I am thankful for ....................................................................

..........................................................................................................


Date .................................. I Love ................................................

..........................................................................................................

I am thankful for ....................................................................

..........................................................................................................


Date .................................. I Love ................................................

..........................................................................................................

I am thankful for ....................................................................

..........................................................................................................


Creative Fusion Journals ©

*Date* .................................. *I Love* ..............................................

..................................................................................................

*I am thankful for* ..................................................................

..................................................................................................


*Date* .................................. *I Love* ..............................................

..................................................................................................

*I am thankful for* ..................................................................

..................................................................................................


*Date* .................................. *I Love* ..............................................

..................................................................................................

*I am thankful for* ..................................................................

..................................................................................................


*Date* .................................. *I Love* ..............................................

..................................................................................................

*I am thankful for* ..................................................................

..................................................................................................

*My Reflections on the week* ...............................................

..................................................................................................

..................................................................................................

Creative Fusion Journals ©

# Begin Your Day with Love & Gratitude

> *The essence of philosophy is that a man should so live that his happiness shall depend as little as possible on external things.*
> *Epictetus*

Date ............................... I Love ................................................

..............................................................................................

I am thankful for ..........................................................................

..............................................................................................

Date ............................... I Love ................................................

..............................................................................................

I am thankful for ..........................................................................

..............................................................................................

Date ............................... I Love ................................................

..............................................................................................

I am thankful for ..........................................................................

..............................................................................................

Creative Fusion Journals ©

Date ................................ I Love ...............................................

..............................................................................................

I am thankful for ...........................................................

..............................................................................................

Date ................................ I Love ...............................................

..............................................................................................

I am thankful for ...........................................................

..............................................................................................

Date ................................ I Love ...............................................

..............................................................................................

I am thankful for ...........................................................

..............................................................................................

Date ................................ I Love ...............................................

..............................................................................................

I am thankful for ...........................................................

..............................................................................................

My Reflections on the week ............................................

..............................................................................................

..............................................................................................

Creative Fusion Journals ©

# Begin Your Day with Love & Gratitude

> *Happiness lies in the joy of achievement and the thrill of creative effort. - Eleanor Roosevelt*
> *~ Acknowledge your own creativity ~*

Date ............................... I Love ...............................................

.....................................................................................................

I am thankful for ...........................................................................

.....................................................................................................

Date ............................... I Love ...............................................

.....................................................................................................

I am thankful for ...........................................................................

.....................................................................................................

Date ............................... I Love ...............................................

.....................................................................................................

I am thankful for ...........................................................................

.....................................................................................................

Creative Fusion Journals ©

*Date* ................................ *I Love* ..............................................................

................................................................................................................

*I am thankful for* ..............................................................................

................................................................................................................

*Date* ................................ *I Love* ..............................................................

................................................................................................................

*I am thankful for* ..............................................................................

................................................................................................................

*Date* ................................ *I Love* ..............................................................

................................................................................................................

*I am thankful for* ..............................................................................

................................................................................................................

*Date* ................................ *I Love* ..............................................................

................................................................................................................

*I am thankful for* ..............................................................................

................................................................................................................

*My Reflections on the week* ..............................................................

................................................................................................................

................................................................................................................

Creative Fusion Journals ©

## Begin Your Day with Love & Gratitude

> *Think only of the positive, say what you believe and do what you know is right. This is the route to contentment & peace.*
> *Ash Azalea*

Date ............................... I Love ................................................
................................................................................................

I am thankful for .....................................................................
................................................................................................

Date ............................... I Love ................................................
................................................................................................

I am thankful for .....................................................................
................................................................................................

Date ............................... I Love ................................................
................................................................................................

I am thankful for .....................................................................
................................................................................................

Creative Fusion Journals ©

*Date* ................................ *I Love* ................................................

............................................................................................

*I am thankful for* ............................................................

............................................................................................

*Date* ................................ *I Love* ................................................

............................................................................................

*I am thankful for* ............................................................

............................................................................................

*Date* ................................ *I Love* ................................................

............................................................................................

*I am thankful for* ............................................................

............................................................................................

*Date* ................................ *I Love* ................................................

............................................................................................

*I am thankful for* ............................................................

............................................................................................

*My Reflections on the week* ............................................................

............................................................................................

............................................................................................

Creative Fusion Journals ©

## Begin Your Day with Love & Gratitude

> *The greatest happiness is to love and be loved.*
> *George Sands*

Date .............................. I Love ..............................

..............................................................................

I am thankful for ..............................................

..............................................................................

Date .............................. I Love ..............................

..............................................................................

I am thankful for ..............................................

..............................................................................

Date .............................. I Love ..............................

..............................................................................

I am thankful for ..............................................

..............................................................................

Creative Fusion Journals ©

*Date* ................................. *I Love* ..................................................

..............................................................................................................

*I am thankful for* ...............................................................................

..............................................................................................................


*Date* ................................. *I Love* ..................................................

..............................................................................................................

*I am thankful for* ...............................................................................

..............................................................................................................


*Date* ................................. *I Love* ..................................................

..............................................................................................................

*I am thankful for* ...............................................................................

..............................................................................................................


*Date* ................................. *I Love* ..................................................

..............................................................................................................

*I am thankful for* ...............................................................................

..............................................................................................................

*My Reflections on the week* ................................................................

..............................................................................................................

..............................................................................................................

Creative Fusion Journals ©

# Begin Your Day with Love & Gratitude

> *Who is the happier, those who braved the storm of life and lived or those who stayed securely on shore and merely existed?*
> *Hunter S Thomson*

Date ............................... I Love ...............................................

..............................................................................................

I am thankful for .........................................................................

..............................................................................................

Date ............................... I Love ...............................................

..............................................................................................

I am thankful for .........................................................................

..............................................................................................

Date ............................... I Love ...............................................

..............................................................................................

I am thankful for .........................................................................

..............................................................................................

Creative Fusion Journals ©

*Date* ............................... *I Love* ..............................................

..............................................................................................

*I am thankful for* ....................................................................

..............................................................................................

*Date* ............................... *I Love* ..............................................

..............................................................................................

*I am thankful for* ....................................................................

..............................................................................................

*Date* ............................... *I Love* ..............................................

..............................................................................................

*I am thankful for* ....................................................................

..............................................................................................

*Date* ............................... *I Love* ..............................................

..............................................................................................

*I am thankful for* ....................................................................

..............................................................................................

*My Reflections on the week* ....................................................

..............................................................................................

..............................................................................................

Creative Fusion Journals ©

# Begin Your Day with Love & Gratitude

> *Nothing ventured nothing gained. So be brave and take calculated risks.*
> *Ash Azalea*

Date ............................... I Love ...............................................

..................................................................................................

I am thankful for ............................................................

..................................................................................................


Date ............................... I Love ...............................................

..................................................................................................

I am thankful for ............................................................

..................................................................................................


Date ............................... I Love ...............................................

..................................................................................................

I am thankful for ............................................................

..................................................................................................

Creative Fusion Journals ©

*Date* ............................... *I Love* ..............................................

..................................................................................................

*I am thankful for* ..................................................................

..................................................................................................

*Date* ............................... *I Love* ..............................................

..................................................................................................

*I am thankful for* ..................................................................

..................................................................................................

*Date* ............................... *I Love* ..............................................

..................................................................................................

*I am thankful for* ..................................................................

..................................................................................................

*Date* ............................... *I Love* ..............................................

..................................................................................................

*I am thankful for* ..................................................................

..................................................................................................

*My Reflections on the week* ................................................

..................................................................................................

..................................................................................................

Creative Fusion Journals ©

# Begin Your Day with Love & Gratitude

> *You cannot protect yourself from sadness without protecting yourself from happiness.*
> *Jonathan Safran Foer*
> *~ So, open your heart to the world ~*

Date ............................... I Love ...............................................

..........................................................................................

I am thankful for ....................................................................

..........................................................................................

Date ............................... I Love ...............................................

..........................................................................................

I am thankful for ....................................................................

..........................................................................................

Date ............................... I Love ...............................................

..........................................................................................

I am thankful for ....................................................................

..........................................................................................

Creative Fusion Journals ©

*Date* .............................. *I Love* ..............................................

............................................................................................................

*I am thankful for* ...................................................................................

............................................................................................................

*Date* .............................. *I Love* ..............................................

............................................................................................................

*I am thankful for* ...................................................................................

............................................................................................................

*Date* .............................. *I Love* ..............................................

............................................................................................................

*I am thankful for* ...................................................................................

............................................................................................................

*Date* .............................. *I Love* ..............................................

............................................................................................................

*I am thankful for* ...................................................................................

............................................................................................................

*My Reflections on the week* ....................................................................

............................................................................................................

............................................................................................................

Creative Fusion Journals ©

# Begin Your Day with Love & Gratitude

> *You yourself, as much as anyone in the universe, deserves your love & affection.*
> *Buddha*
> *~ Love Yourself ~*

Date ............................... I Love ..............................................

............................................................................................

I am thankful for ......................................................................

............................................................................................

Date ............................... I Love ..............................................

............................................................................................

I am thankful for ......................................................................

............................................................................................

Date ............................... I Love ..............................................

............................................................................................

I am thankful for ......................................................................

............................................................................................

Creative Fusion Journals ©

*Date* ............................... *I Love* ..........................................................

............................................................................................................

*I am thankful for* .......................................................................................

............................................................................................................

*Date* ............................... *I Love* ..........................................................

............................................................................................................

*I am thankful for* .......................................................................................

............................................................................................................

*Date* ............................... *I Love* ..........................................................

............................................................................................................

*I am thankful for* .......................................................................................

............................................................................................................

*Date* ............................... *I Love* ..........................................................

............................................................................................................

*I am thankful for* .......................................................................................

............................................................................................................

*My Reflections on the week* ........................................................................

............................................................................................................

............................................................................................................

Creative Fusion Journals ©

## Begin Your Day with Love & Gratitude

> *The deeper you love yourself, the more the universe will affirm your worth.*
> *Alan Cohen*
> *~ Love Yourself ~*

Date .................................. I Love ..............................................

...........................................................................................

I am thankful for .........................................................................

...........................................................................................


Date .................................. I Love ..............................................

...........................................................................................

I am thankful for .........................................................................

...........................................................................................


Date .................................. I Love ..............................................

...........................................................................................

I am thankful for .........................................................................

...........................................................................................

Creative Fusion Journals ©

*Date* .................................. *I Love* .................................................................

..............................................................................................................................

*I am thankful for* ......................................................................................................

..............................................................................................................................

*Date* .................................. *I Love* .................................................................

..............................................................................................................................

*I am thankful for* ......................................................................................................

..............................................................................................................................

*Date* .................................. *I Love* .................................................................

..............................................................................................................................

*I am thankful for* ......................................................................................................

..............................................................................................................................

*Date* .................................. *I Love* .................................................................

..............................................................................................................................

*I am thankful for* ......................................................................................................

..............................................................................................................................

*My Reflections on the week* .....................................................................................

..............................................................................................................................

..............................................................................................................................

Creative Fusion Journals ©

## Begin Your Day with Love & Gratitude

> *Loving yourself isn't vanity. It's sanity.*
> *Katrina Mayer*
> *~ Love Yourself ~*

Date ............................... I Love ...............................................

..............................................................................................

I am thankful for .......................................................................

..............................................................................................


Date ............................... I Love ...............................................

..............................................................................................

I am thankful for .......................................................................

..............................................................................................


Date ............................... I Love ...............................................

..............................................................................................

I am thankful for .......................................................................

..............................................................................................

Creative Fusion Journals ©

Date ............................... I Love .............................................
...................................................................................................
I am thankful for ...........................................................
...................................................................................................

Date ............................... I Love .............................................
...................................................................................................
I am thankful for ...........................................................
...................................................................................................

Date ............................... I Love .............................................
...................................................................................................
I am thankful for ...........................................................
...................................................................................................

Date ............................... I Love .............................................
...................................................................................................
I am thankful for ...........................................................
...................................................................................................
My Reflections on the week ...........................................
...................................................................................................
...................................................................................................

Creative Fusion Journals ©

## Begin Your Day with Love & Gratitude

> *Self-love is an ocean and your heart is a vessel. Make it full, and any excess will spill over into the lives of the people you hold dear. But you must come first.*
> *Beau Taplin*

Date ................................ I Love ................................................

............................................................................................................

I am thankful for ...........................................................................

............................................................................................................

Date ................................ I Love ................................................

............................................................................................................

I am thankful for ...........................................................................

............................................................................................................

Date ................................ I Love ................................................

............................................................................................................

I am thankful for ...........................................................................

............................................................................................................

Creative Fusion Journals ©

Date ................................. I Love ..............................................

................................................................................................

I am thankful for ............................................................

................................................................................................


Date ................................. I Love ..............................................

................................................................................................

I am thankful for ............................................................

................................................................................................


Date ................................. I Love ..............................................

................................................................................................

I am thankful for ............................................................

................................................................................................


Date ................................. I Love ..............................................

................................................................................................

I am thankful for ............................................................

................................................................................................

My Reflections on the week ............................................

................................................................................................

................................................................................................

Creative Fusion Journals ©

## Begin Your Day with Love & Gratitude

*You can not do a kindness too soon because you never know how soon it will be too late.*
*Ralph Waldo Amiel*

Date ............................... I Love ...............................................

................................................................................................

I am thankful for .............................................................

................................................................................................


Date ............................... I Love ...............................................

................................................................................................

I am thankful for .............................................................

................................................................................................


Date ............................... I Love ...............................................

................................................................................................

I am thankful for .............................................................

................................................................................................


Creative Fusion Journals ©

*Date* .................................. *I Love* ..............................................

................................................................................................................

*I am thankful for* ...........................................................................

................................................................................................................

*Date* .................................. *I Love* ..............................................

................................................................................................................

*I am thankful for* ...........................................................................

................................................................................................................

*Date* .................................. *I Love* ..............................................

................................................................................................................

*I am thankful for* ...........................................................................

................................................................................................................

*Date* .................................. *I Love* ..............................................

................................................................................................................

*I am thankful for* ...........................................................................

................................................................................................................

*My Reflections on the week* ...........................................................

................................................................................................................

................................................................................................................

Creative Fusion Journals ©

## Begin Your Day with Love & Gratitude

> *The sea of life is at times calm and other times stormy. Prepare for the storms, so you can enjoy the calm secure in the knowledge of readiness.*
> *Ash Azalea*

Date ............................. I Love ...........................................

................................................................................

I am thankful for ..........................................................

................................................................................

Date ............................. I Love ...........................................

................................................................................

I am thankful for ..........................................................

................................................................................

Date ............................. I Love ...........................................

................................................................................

I am thankful for ..........................................................

................................................................................

Creative Fusion Journals ©

*Date* ............................... *I Love* ..........................................................

...................................................................................................................

*I am thankful for* ...............................................................................

...................................................................................................................

*Date* ............................... *I Love* ..........................................................

...................................................................................................................

*I am thankful for* ...............................................................................

...................................................................................................................

*Date* ............................... *I Love* ..........................................................

...................................................................................................................

*I am thankful for* ...............................................................................

...................................................................................................................

*Date* ............................... *I Love* ..........................................................

...................................................................................................................

*I am thankful for* ...............................................................................

...................................................................................................................

*My Reflections on the week* ..............................................................

...................................................................................................................

...................................................................................................................

Creative Fusion Journals ©

# Begin Your Day with Love & Gratitude

> *Put yourself in a state of mind where you say, 'Here is an opportunity for me to celebrate my own power, my ability to do whatever is necessary.'.*
> *Martin Luther King*

Date ................................ I Love ...............................................

................................................................................................

I am thankful for ................................................................

................................................................................................

Date ................................ I Love ...............................................

................................................................................................

I am thankful for ................................................................

................................................................................................

Date ................................ I Love ...............................................

................................................................................................

I am thankful for ................................................................

................................................................................................

Creative Fusion Journals ©

Date ................................ I Love ................................................

................................................................................................

I am thankful for ..................................................................

................................................................................................

Date ................................ I Love ................................................

................................................................................................

I am thankful for ..................................................................

................................................................................................

Date ................................ I Love ................................................

................................................................................................

I am thankful for ..................................................................

................................................................................................

Date ................................ I Love ................................................

................................................................................................

I am thankful for ..................................................................

................................................................................................

My Reflections on the week ................................................................

................................................................................................

................................................................................................

Creative Fusion Journals ©

## Begin Your Day with Love & Gratitude

> *Life is not a mountain to conquer, but a challenging journey offering opportunity every day along the way.*
> Ash Azalea

Date ............................... I Love ...............................................

..................................................................................................

I am thankful for ...........................................................................

..................................................................................................


Date ............................... I Love ...............................................

..................................................................................................

I am thankful for ...........................................................................

..................................................................................................


Date ............................... I Love ...............................................

..................................................................................................

I am thankful for ...........................................................................

..................................................................................................


Creative Fusion Journals ©

*Date* .................................. *I Love* ....................................................................

............................................................................................................................

*I am thankful for* ................................................................................................

............................................................................................................................

*Date* .................................. *I Love* ....................................................................

............................................................................................................................

*I am thankful for* ................................................................................................

............................................................................................................................

*Date* .................................. *I Love* ....................................................................

............................................................................................................................

*I am thankful for* ................................................................................................

............................................................................................................................

*Date* .................................. *I Love* ....................................................................

............................................................................................................................

*I am thankful for* ................................................................................................

............................................................................................................................

*My Reflections on the week* ................................................................................

............................................................................................................................

............................................................................................................................

Creative Fusion Journals ©

*Monthly Reflections*

*Put aside some time at the end of each month to review your reflections and see if there is a particular direction for your love, thankfulness and personal growth. Think how you might develop and strengthen your positive perspectives.*

..............................................................................
..............................................................................
..............................................................................
..............................................................................
..............................................................................
..............................................................................
..............................................................................
..............................................................................
..............................................................................
..............................................................................
..............................................................................
..............................................................................
..............................................................................
..............................................................................
..............................................................................
..............................................................................
..............................................................................
..............................................................................
..............................................................................

Creative Fusion Journals ©

Creative Fusion Journals ©

Creative Fusion Journals ©

Creative Fusion Journals ©

# End of the Journal Reflections

Now your Journal is completed, as you have each week and month, set aside some quality time to quietly review your entries and reflect on the love and gratitude in your life and your journey of personal growth.

...........................................................................
...........................................................................
...........................................................................
...........................................................................
...........................................................................
...........................................................................
...........................................................................
...........................................................................
...........................................................................
...........................................................................
...........................................................................
...........................................................................
...........................................................................
...........................................................................
...........................................................................
...........................................................................
...........................................................................
...........................................................................

Creative Fusion Journals ©

*Share your love*

~ ~ ~

*Show your gratitude*

Creative Fusion Journals ©

Printed by Amazon Italia Logistica S.r.l.
Torrazza Piemonte (TO), Italy